THE LIVES OF MINIBEASTS

Busy BEES

By Holly Duhig

©2017
Book Life
King's Lynn
Norfolk PE30 4LS

ISBN: 978-1-78637-185-0

Written by:
Holly Duhig

Edited by:
Charlie Ogden

Designed by:
Danielle Jones

A catalogue record for this book
is available from the British Library

Photo Credits

CONTENTS

Page 4	What Is a Bee?
Page 6	What Does a Bee Look Like?
Page 8	How Do Bees Lay Eggs?
Page 10	Bee Larvae
Page 12	Where Do Bees Live?
Page 14	What Do Bees Eat?
Page 16	What Do Bees Do?
Page 18	How Do Bees Help?
Page 20	Busy Bees
Page 22	Fun Facts
Page 24	Glossary and Index

Words that look like **this** can be found in the glossary on page 24.

WHAT IS A BEE?

Bee

A bee is an insect with six legs and small wings. Bees live in hives with lots of other bees and one queen bee.

Honeybees make honey to feed themselves and their **young**. Bees make more honey than they can eat, so people can collect and eat their honey too.

Honey

WHAT DOES A BEE LOOK LIKE?

Stripes

Eyes

Antennae

Bees' bodies are covered in black and yellow stripes. Bees have five eyes and two antennae. They use their antennae to smell, which can help them to find flowers.

Female bees are called worker bees and male bees are called drones. Drones are bigger than workers, but the biggest bee in the hive is always the queen bee.

Queen

Worker

Drone

There can only be one queen bee in a hive.

HOW DO BEES LAY EGGS?

The queen bee will leave the hive to find a **mate**. This will be a drone from a different hive. Once she has found a mate, she is able to lay eggs.

Bees make lots of **hexagons** out of wax. This is called honeycomb. Each hexagon is called a cell. The queen bee lays her eggs in the cells. The eggs hatch and become **larvae**.

Bee Larvae in Honeycomb

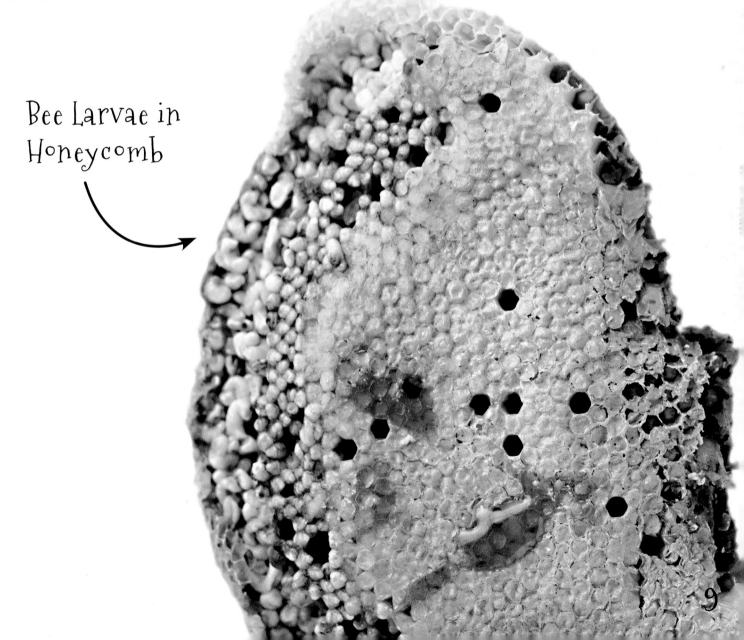

9

BEE LARVAE

The larvae are fed **royal jelly**. After a while, they are fed honey instead. Only larvae that might become queen bees are still fed royal jelly.

In order for a larva to turn into a bee, its cell must be sealed closed with wax. Inside the cell, the larva's body body slowly changes into that of a bee.

Queens emerge from the honeycomb after just 16 days, but other bees take between 21 and 24 days.

WHERE DO BEES LIVE?

Natural Hive

Bees live in a hive. **Natural** hives are usually found in trees. Bees make these hives using beeswax.

Bees' bodies make wax when they eat honey. They chew the wax until it is soft and then use it to build their hives.

Beeswax can be used to make candles!

WHAT DO BEES EAT?

Bees eat the honey that they make. Bees make honey by drinking nectar from flowers. Nectar is a sugary liquid that flowers make to **attract** insects.

14

Back in the hive, the bees pass the nectar between one another using their mouths. This sucks all the water out of the nectar and turns it into honey.

WHAT DO BEES DO?

This swarm of bees is resting in a tree.

Bees are known for their swarms. Swarms are groups of bees that leave one hive to find a new hive. Swarms happen when a hive gets too big.

When a hive is too big, some of the bees don't realise they have a queen and they start to raise a new one. The true queen must leave before she is replaced!

Swarms can include up to 30,000 bees!

HOW DO BEES HELP?

Bees help new plants and flowers to grow. When a bee drinks nectar from a flower, the flower's **pollen** sticks to its body.

The bee carries this pollen to the next flower it lands on.
This flower then uses the pollen to make new seeds.
New seeds eventually grow into new plants and flowers.

BUSY BEES

Africanised
Honeybee

Africanised honeybees are known for being angry!
They sting in large groups and have been known
to chase people.

Kufra honeybees live in the desert! They make their hives near **oases** where there are plenty of flowers.

FUN FACTS

Honeybees have stings to help protect their hive, but as soon as they have stung a person, they will die.

Worker bees only live for around six weeks, but queen bees can live for up to five years!

Bees can flap their wings 190 times in one second! It is this fast flapping that makes the buzzing sound that bees are known for.

A queen bee can lay up to 2,500 eggs in one day!

23

GLOSSARY

attract	cause to come closer
hexagons	shapes with six equal sides
larvae	young insects that must grow and change before they can reach their adult forms
mate	a member of the same species that an animal has young with
natural	found in nature, not man-made
oases	places in the desert where water is found
pollen	a powder-like substance made by plants
royal jelly	a substance made by bees to feed their young
young	the offspring of animals

INDEX

beeswax 12–13

cells 9, 11

drones 7–8

honey 5, 10, 13–15

honeycomb 9, 11

larvae 9–11

legs 4

nectar 14–15, 18

pollen 18–19

royal jelly 10

wings 4, 23

workers 7, 22